Everything:
New and Selected Poems

by
Terry Lucas

Blue Light Press ◆ 1st World Publishing

San Francisco ◆ Fairfield ◆ Delhi

Winner of the 2025 Blue Light Book Award

Everything: New and Selected Poems

Copyright ©2025 by Terry Lucas

All rights reserved. Printed in the United States of America. No part of this book may be used or reproduced in any manner whatsoever without written permission except in the case of brief quotations embodied in critical articles and reviews. For information contact:

1st World Library
PO Box 2211
Fairfield, IA 52556
www.1stworldpublishing.com

Blue Light Press
www.bluelightpress.com
bluelightpress@aol.com

Book & Cover Design
Melanie Gendron
melaniegendron999@gmail.com

Cover Art
Jim Benton

Author Photo
Tayve Neese

First Edition

Library of Congress Cataloging-in-Publication Data

ISBN: 978-1-4218-3573-0

Everything:
New And Selected Poems

Suspects

We're gathered here to make these poems talk,
grill them under hot lights, long chains swaying
bare bulbs above us, shadows washing stains
from concrete floors, cracks of gauzy light
beneath locked doors. We're here to lay them out,
strip them down to naked lines, slap veins till gorged,
pump them full of truth serum, ask twenty questions,
get confessions – how bright the blood,
how dark the bathwater, how they broke in
through the skylight, escaped leaving no tracks
in virgin snow. How they were captured –
how many hands were laid upon them
before they sang.

Table of Contents

Proem: Suspects v

from *Altar Call*

The Spell 1
Prayer Meeting with Folding Chair 3
Cushion 4
Midwatch 6
Lesson 8
Phaseolus Lunatis 9
What I Learned from My Mother 10
The Call 11

from *If They Have Ears to Hear*

The Augur's Prayer 15
Some Days I Find Myself 16
Black Friday 18
Wedding Cravat 19
Final Fitting Appointment 20
Closing Time 21
Tonight 22
Deus Ex Machina 23
If They Have Ears to Hear 24

from *In This Room*

In This Room 27
Wind 28
Addicted 29
1967 30
Appointment 31
Witness 32
Spoils 34
Break 35

American-Amicable Life 36
Dream Ending with a Line By Charles Wright 38
Nightshade 39
The Gate (prologue and sections 1-11) 41

from *Dharma Rain*

Vortices 61
Horse Latitudes 62
A Short History of Baby Incubators 63
Swords, Seed, Gods, & Gold 64
When God Moved Out 66
Psalm '66 67
Meet Calvin 68
He Couldn't Play in Dance Band Because Dancing Was a Sin .. 69
Love Lifted Him Not 70
Dharma Rain 71
Spirit 75
Recycling 76
To the Fog 78

from *The Thing Itself*

Neighbors at 2 a.m. 81
Morning Ritual 82
By Any Other Name 83
Safeway 84
I never wanted to be a poet 85
Shiprock 86
New Mexico Sighting 87
Dear Frogs of Pinckneyville, Illinois 88
Slow Dancing 90
A Small Pebble 91
All roads 93
The Thing Itself (A Cento) 94

Everything: New Poems

Cento with a Few Old Books Thrown In 97
Refusal with Broken Wheel 98
Sheltering in Place with Steely Dan 99
My Father Draws His Colt .45 for the Final Time 100
Upright 101
Break Room 103
Intermission 104
Black Suns 105
Dearborn Street 107
The Past 109
Room Therapy 110
Desktop Cento 111
Everything 112
Erasure Ending in the Sound of Sweet Nothing 113

Acknowledgments 115
Notes 117
About the Author 121

from
ALTAR CALL

The Spell

> *Beware of false prophets, which come to you in sheep's clothing,
> but inwardly they are ravening wolves.*
> – Matthew 7:15 KJV

By age seven, I was smitten
with God, seduced and turned
into one of his sheep. At prayer meetings,

I made *special requests* –
for Brother Valley West's phantom
arm to stop aching, for the doctors

giving Sister Katherine shock treatments
in the asylum to be filled with Holy Ghost
healing power – and the entire congregation

would come round after the benediction,
hugging and kissing me on the mouth,
wanting a taste of the red coal

Brother Swinford said God had touched
to my lips as He had to Isaiah's. It was true,
the spell was good enough for me to preach

my first sermon at eleven, earn an advanced degree
in religion, spend half a lifetime in fumbling
foreplay with God, trying so hard in the dark

to feel some bulge under all those layers, straining
for release from bituminous desire, tongue
glowing just below the flash point

of faith's flame. And later, I understood
the white ash in the corners of my mouth, the cooling
slake of thirst. But now, I really don't know

what to make of that spell, how it entered me
like an abusive shepherd who all along must have known
there would come a day of judgment, and a night before

when the first tufts of wolf fur showed through the wool.

Prayer Meeting with Folding Chair

Cancer mainly, it was cancer and the occasional car accident
That pulled the small band of church members down

Into the basement Wednesday nights, caused women to rest
Foreheads in palms, men to crouch on the scuffed linoleum floor,

Grip the back of a gray metal folding chair as fiercely as a child
Steadying a wooden ladder, fearing the father

Standing on rickety steps unscrewing a burned-out light bulb
Might fall – cancer and the covered Corning Ware dishes cooling

Drew them to prayer meeting. The coffeemaker's unblinking red
Light, pure water vapor separating and rising like a spirit,

Leaving behind a sludge turning dark and bitter on the burner,
Forming a skin thick enough to support particles of dust

And small flying insects drowning in Styrofoam cups.
The coal oil furnace, even the gas stove called them in

From the high desert winter that slipped under doors like sand –
That was sand, sand bleached of summer, bleached of every season,

A sand that eagerly stripped momentum from an out-of-control car
Leaving passengers alone to deal with objects in its path, a whirling

Pillar of sand falling from clouds, drifting across roads branching
Like veins on maps in their bodies, burying populations carried there –

Down in the basement – a limp blue glove, the gauzy smudge
Of a palm on the cold back of a gray metal folding chair.

Cushion

Breath whistling through nacreous teeth, my father laughed
telling the story of an Interstate Commerce man pulling him over,
claiming the tires on his 18-wheeler weren't touching pavement
at 80 mph in marbled rain. Half-bald and gibbous with gray

dust, the worn-out Goodyear husks leaned against bare studs
framing our garage, like aging veterans on our corner grocery store
porch – out of work and low on credit with old man Edwards,
my father would drag them back into active duty. One by one,

I'd roll them down the driveway like invalids
wheeled into the lobby of the Aztec Ruins Museum,
wait inside the pickup cab, try to rub off the stain
penetrating lines of my hands, while my father sang

each corpse into the bed with a grunt, climbed in and pushed
the silver button that cranked up the flat-head V-8. Starting
with the old Sinclair at the Y, we'd make the rounds,
work our way to La Plata Highway, stopping at all the garages,

ask if they were buying, what outfits might be hiring,
ending up at the junkyard where Big Al was always good
for 25 cents a carcass – sometimes we'd go home
with enough quarters to make a roll, but most often

just the few dollars my father would hand my mother,
minus bills held back for the drive-in movie that night.
Feet propped on the heater under the dash, I'd smell the hot chrome
cup unscrewed from the top of my father's green Stanley thermos,

slurp black coffee past salty lips to dance on blistered tongue
before my father poured in Southern Comfort. When the wind-
shield fogged, I'd wipe cold glass with bare hands,
rub them together, feel the sticky residue of rubber, think

if we could just go fast enough, I might never have to touch the rain.

Midwatch

> *In the military, midwatch is the four-hour watch from midnight to 4:00 a.m.*

If I sit perfectly still
    in this room, can I tell
        midnight from morrow?

In the dark, I believe
    the red and purple fists
        of unopened four o'clocks,

the midwatch
    of my mother's coffee pot,
        stories that bubble up

the metal throat, sobbing their way
    through curved glass lid, her lips
        swollen with memory of the blaze.

If I ask her how
    she stays up for the eclipse
        of my father, her answer is a rustling

sound of a wren pushing its young
    from the nest, trusting metal-flecked bones
        to line up with true north,

the way iron shavings gather
    around magnetic poles below the surface
        of a page. Which way to go? North? Or farther

into my father? If I cling
    to the edge, will I hear a fist clench
        before it strikes the hour, sounding the alarm?

I ask my mother again,
    When will the watch end?
        I listen for metal in the marrow,

only hear old water whisper,
    bargaining with blue flames below....

Lesson

My father once broke a man's tailbone
With the toe of his roach killer boot
For having an American flag
Sewn onto the seat of his jeans.
Doctors dug denim from his rectum,
Stars from his colon, kept him
In the hospital. My father paid him
A visit, gave him a Bible and a history lesson –
North Africa, Sicily, Anzio, Salerno –
Told him why he didn't like the places
Some people put the flag his buddies died for.
My father left a blank check at the front desk,
Pointed his White Freightliner west, depressed
The accelerator with his freshly spit-shined boot –
Spider-veined with scars that would never buff out.

Phaseolus Lunatis

My mother's ER bag was always packed
And sitting at the front door when I cooked
Butter beans which, she swore, were poisonous
Undercooked. Every emergency room
Doctor in San Juan County Hospital
Knew her burgeoning phobia, every
Nurse the name, *Phaseolus Lunatis,*
Written on the white label stuck to a
Ziploc plastic-bagged sample of my beans –
Snap, green, wax, kidney – it made no difference
What species, they had to be boiled to mush
In a lidded pot, drained and reheated
In fresh water – if not, the cramps began,
Accusations that I was trying to
Kill her again, the *get a sample of*
The poison beans, I'm getting my bag
And heading to the car conversation.
In the waiting room for an hour or more,
Mother lying behind closed curtains,
Always the same report back from the lab:
Negative. When we told her, she'd get out
Of bed, dress, go home – later open up
That bag, take out housecoat, gown, bottles, vials,
Repack it all, freight it to the front closet,
Then ask for something to eat – *May I please*
Have a plate of some nice mushy beans?

What I Learned from My Mother

I learned from my mother how to worry
What all the neighbors would think, to close up
Storm windows when my father was yelling
And putting practiced fists through doors. To kill
Difficult emotions with my bare thoughts,
Only letting the stubborn ones escape
Through a migraine headache. To hold my breath,
My tongue, my bowel movements. To let each
Present moment slip away in favor
Of a future heaven or perfection
Hell – I learned from my mother how to talk
The talk, without ever believing it
Myself. But mostly what I learned from her
Was how to teach her grandchildren well.

The Call

When my father dies, I am one thousand miles away
from his heart, beating both iambic and trochaic at once,

syncopated whispers coming through my hands-
free earpiece: *This thing just shocked me,*

I hear him tell the night desk nurse,
who later described the slow slump, defibrillator

dangling from his neck, swaying in blank air.

But right now, all I can hear are her feverish steps
on linoleum floor, muddy speech of emergency

paramedics, cellular silence – and God
there is nowhere to get off this mountain road,

each switchback demanding full attention
in the moonless night. Later in my hotel room,

after speaking for the final time with the doctor,
I am ten again, on my knees, stranded

on a seal-black boulder in the middle of the Animas
River, reaching for the out of reach

arms of my father. *Pick a spot on shore,* he says,
to focus on. I place one hand on a rock offering

itself through the swirling surface. I pause,
then push off toward the fog gathered around the dead

limbs nodding in shallows, still attached
to cottonwoods. Legs pumping, my submerged hands

part black water like an orchestra conductor
cutting off the woodwinds at the end of an adagio,

air barely moving over humming reeds,
a sustained tone with no apparent rhythm,

asymptotically arcing its way towards a measureless fermata.

from
If They Have Ears to Hear

The Augur's Prayer

If I speak for God's silence, I must dance
Inside my mother's womb, my tongue

Growing inside her, a flaming root
Pushing through humus. I must

Fill my cheeks with Father's arid breath,
Nurse from his dry breasts.

If I speak for God's silence, I must rest
Inside stones lining His son's triumphal entrance.

I must scatter myself like seed carried away by wrens
Or else feed like hawks on the flesh of thieves

Hanging on Golgotha, stripped carcasses of men –
Wings for faces.

Some Days I Find Myself

Some days I find myself
sitting at my desk
fifteen minutes without thinking
about death –
                      or about the Sun,
the feverish Sun hoisting itself up
eucalyptus trees outside my window,
how its malignancy even now is growing
plasma tsunamis –
                      how one day flaming
waves will engulf the entire family
of squirrels racing along wrinkled bark,
dolphins, elephants, bees –
                      every violin
will scream as music melts,
along with all the crumbled roads,
massive missives written from sagging motel beds,
golden Gideon Bibles, packages of Trojans,
buzzing neon signs, naked candles dancing
behind luminarias' parchment,
                      curled up
shoes in Salvation Army stores.
But, tonight I simply watch
Earth's thin shadow cross
the Moon, the way a child
sitting at the dinner table watches
his abused mother's face,
                      half-lit
pockmarked scars shining like craters,
waiting for the father's eclipse.

And now it's sleeting in the streetlights,
ice particles sighing through spaces
                      in the spaces

before white noise hits cement like tongues
against teeth, or fists against a whorled-grained desk,
and once again I find myself
thinking –
        not so much about death,
but the sound of claws skittering up eucalyptus,
fellow fugitives from the star that gave us birth,
even now flexing flaring arms –
                              to embrace us.

Black Friday

At 6 a.m. I turn into the mall parking lot, steer around
speed bumps, nose the Accord into its reserved spot. Already

sticks of manicured coppice are blushing muted rose
and sage. Already, light is pooling on car hoods, graying

roofs over The Gap, Victoria's Secret, Starbucks, opening up
to cathedral space, where *the closer I get to you,*

the more you make me see is looping endlessly between
food courts and anchor stores. Outside, customers

press against smudged glass doors, pale envelopes
of coupons and double-bonus dollars in their fists. I crack

the car door and twist both feet to work my Allen-Edmond wingtips
from floorboard to pavement without scuffing mirrored toes.

See my body follow with measured obedience, slip through
hordes, lift the grated metal gate to my tailored clothing store, enter

code to deactivate the alarm – then disappear
behind a wall of worsted wool, a flicker of the artificial

lights before they catch. See me emerge, translucent
plastic tubes of coins and rubber-banded bills in hand,

count the drawers, reach inside my triple-pleated trouser pocket,
pull out keys, walk to the door, extend my hand,

welcome you into the maw of America.

Wedding Cravat

They were reverential customers –
her whispering in the funereal

voice of a mourner, intoning *not
cinnabar. What do you think*

about vermilion? His measured pace
around the tie boat as solemn

as any viewing of the departed,
waiting for a flutter of the eyelash-

thin thread, or some other signal resting
squarely upon the liminal, undecided

which way to fall: with or against
prevailing winds. *How do you tie a knot?*

he thought. *And what's the difference
between full and half*

Windsors? Single overhand is the easiest,
his father always said. *Besides,*

they all come untied in the end.

Final Fitting Appointment

Another customer in the five-way mirror,
André, the tailor, chalking up a two-button,

charcoal, Abboud suit – diagonal ciphers
begin at both armholes, follow tapered sides

down through the double-vented coat's tail,
signaling how much material needs letting out,

how many pounds gained since the wedding.
Tomorrow he will don this drab gabardine for her

funeral. She will be dressed in basic black
forever. The master tailor will take

care in shaping her earthen gown: it will mold
to her body no matter how much weight

lost to maggots, proboscises probing seams
in pleated skin, unweaving flesh like needles

of millions of blind stitch machines gone awry –
their arrhythmic, electric voices even now

calling to the murmuring auricle in his heart.

Closing Time

Second and Market, San Francisco

The comfort of coins echoing in their register
trays: contralto quarters, soprano dimes
chiming the hour above whisper of paper
money – counting down the drawer.

Roy, our assistant manager, shakes off
late customers rattling the door,
eyes never straying from the blinking
cursor on blue crystal display.

Heather and I feather the wall, fingers
grooming limp suit sleeves, coaxing
regimen from remains of the worried
lambskin, cashmere, worsted wool,

after shoppers have had their way.
We work from the store's dark belly
toward well-lighted window displays –
those undead mannequins that stand

guard over capitalism. Then Roy
tells us to get our bags and not to move
while he sets the alarm, says ok,
and we step over the iron gate

runner. He turns the key and tests
the siren, which sounds, as we walk
across the street to the Palace Hotel,
with a slightly different urgency than the first

'96 Grgich Cab gurgling into bubble glasses,
Heather's blue-green eyes blaring into mine.

Tonight

I'll take a glass of wine – a red
rose, turn it inside out,
feel its velvet nose against my ribs
from inside
the cage.

I'll pace
myself,
take a bite
of solid food, something
dead, covered with fried bread,

go back to the red –
I dread the white
granite day, silver
backed suits, blood
ties, pin-striped lines
that never stray – almost

drunk now – between
firm bed-
rock flash of snow-
bladed senses

and marshy bottom
that never shows
its secrets
face up – not quite

sober, not quite
drunk –
in the bluesy, juicy slush
that you just can't trust –
but do.

Deus Ex Machina

I read about a muscle in the thumb
that often twitches below the limen
of perception – no apparent reason
is known. Scientists attached electrodes
to this *pollicis brevis*, hooked them up
to a toggle switch so the subject could control
an unpleasant tone –

                      perhaps it was too loud
a siren, a bad poem recited ad infinitum,
like war. This power in the thumb
electrochemically amplified its frequency
just enough to turn off the shrill pitch.

                      I understand
the experiment, what it was about –
learning below the conscious
mind, finding tender to negotiate
chronic pain.

                      But what about that twitch?
How it first must have gripped an antelope
bone or fashioned flint into spear tips,
drawing blood from its brothers and sisters
that opposed it along the way. How it hitch-
hiked on the back of our genome, while we
drudged through all those millennia.

How it kneeled deep inside us, waiting
for some god to create this *machina*,
so it could rise up, a savior.

If They Have Ears To Hear
For Chicu

A gold-plated phonograph record is coursing
through interstellar space, eleven billion miles
from Earth, a message coiled on its surface.
Forty thousand years from now, if there are inhabitants
in the closest system, they might coax out the voices
of Carl Sagan and Kurt Waldheim, telling
the tale of a species that struck out
against the darkness with fire. These beings
will hear, if they have ears to hear, sounds
of the surf, humpback whales, greetings in Swahili,
Akkadian, and Wu. But of Carthage, My Lai, Berlin –
not a single sour pitch. Nor of Auschwitz,
the ovens, nor that Waldheim was forced to resign
as Secretary-General of the United Nations. On the floor
in Chicago, a poet sits with Waldheim's memoirs, crossing
through words that do not make a poem. Most pages turn
black. The poem is about the poet, the poem is about the voyage
through the dark on a gold-plated record.

from
In This Room

In This Room

A long-playing record is turning on the turntable. For some time,

Speakers have been faithfully amplifying scratches behind Art,

Or Miles, or Freddie, with a metronomic ticking, the needle

Bumping up against the label, sending tonearm veering

Back across the smooth gap like a saxophonist swaying on stage,

Or a drunk driving a black-iced road on a new moon night,

Searching for the centerline – but these are mere musings.

From another room, there might be the moaning

Of lovers over hiss of knees caressing satin sheets.

And who is to say which is more holy? Heaven's music or Hell's

Static electricity? The arm holding the needle in the groove, legs

Rising and falling out of time, moonlight flushing the dry flesh

Of curled leaves blowing across the road tangled in the hills

Like a necklace in my mother's hair fanned out on my father's pillow.

And what am I but the valley between? A watershed of snow melt

And shade. A cry from one far peak to another, an avalanche

Of sound echoing between the walls of yet another room,

Where a trembling index finger is lowering the stylus,

Aiming the needle for the edge of a black vinyl record.

Wind

is what will not stop coming through the windows
all day coming through the doors like children
taking turns playing taps on a leaky bugle not knowing
where the tune comes from keeping me
on the other side of the room by the fire reading
a poet's lines about new mexico about robin
and sally and meredith how long ago
lying beneath robin the high desert sand
in her fists a plastic syringe or a man
with blond hair or my shoulders as she came on top
crying and sally strapping on her six-string to teach me
how to play "california dreamin'" sayin' *don't be afraid
to change chords before you think you're ready* the tracks
on her forearms shifting as she walked up and down the
bass strings or meredith telling her stories over
beer-talk that blew up from the parking lot how she
drank a twelve-pack tried to beat the train and the night
i lifted her out of her wheelchair we did all we could
on the dance floor how they came to be part of a history a
rosary i need to say i don't know why today it's just the wind
will not stop coming through the windows

Addicted
After Gerald Stern

I grew up with diesel in my mouth,
aroma of hobo coffee boiling on the stove,
poured into my father's Stanley thermos –
addicted by age six, I stole
slurpy sips testing the temp
before passing chrome cup
across the doghouse, riding shotgun
in my father's snub-nose cab-over,
his eyes always tending to the road, left
hand on the wheel, right flicking
twin stick shifts, as he ran
the 250 Cummins through the gears,
before taking a swallow of steaming brew,
then passing it back, resting palm on knob
ticking to the rhythm of the toothed transmission – all one song
lifting like a carnival ride, then decelerating
with mechanical whine, entering town
after façade town, fiction after fiction.

1967

After Larry Levis

I hear it mostly in the deep
guttural tailpipes of Fords & Chevys
revving out of a Friday afternoon
high school parking lot in a small New Mexican desert
town – Sunset Avenue pulsing
like a neck vein that leads to the heart
of downtown, where Main Street pumps cars all night
stop light to stop light between the A&W
and the Tastee-Freez, engines overheating
then boiling over in ice-patched 2 a.m.
driveways, cooling down with the ticking sounds
of shrinking metal, re-buckling of belts, re-hooking of bras.

I'd like to talk to those boys behind the wheels,
girls curled up on humps between bucket seats;
I'd like to tell them there is nothing out here
in twenty thirteen except what they bring with them,
how they should climb out and start packing –
juniper's needle-leaves not yet pressed
between pages of a Bible, a scorpion's breath
exhaled through abdominal stigmata, sand swept
from sagebrush roots, lifted by the twisting fist of a dust devil,
all collected in luggaged silence – I'd like to tell them

how there will always be enough falling
brimstone, lakes of fire, flaming bushes,
wilted flowers, how there will always be enough gods
to punish them for putting their tongues to the warm clay,
to turn them to salt for glancing back while walking away,
how, when asked *where are you? what have you done?*
who told you that you were naked? what they will need most
will be to learn to love the questions.

Appointment
3 a.m.

First sleep done.
I sit on my deck, huddled around a coffee cup
giving up its small measure of heat – an agitation
water and dark beans have briefly borrowed
from the Sun, before passing it to palms,
cheeks, lips, gut. And I too
slowly rise and feel the fuel of my flesh
drawn back into the merciless engine of the universe –
the great pistons of Ursa Major, Orion, Hercules, Cepheus
driving the gears of providence or chance or the mystery
whirling between them. I wait for something
to move, change color, blink. Not even a wink.
In the yard below, no gray aliens peer into windows,
no reptilians march up the street rank and file, laser guns
readied in scaly-toed hands. Even the town
crazy who lives next door has deserted her nude lawn
dance, black blades of grass untrampled, erect.
I close my eyes and squint, hoping. But I'm no good
at meditation. I try to focus on my breath, the bulge
in the membrane some say separates this world
from the next. I only see the emptiness
of a church altar, a boy kneeling before candles,
their white, unlit wicks. My cup is nearly empty,
coffee cold. I go inside and start over,
pour new water, twist alive the yellow-spitting flame,
baptize fresh grounds, once more feel the elixir
swimming up my veins, like crazed salmon
returning to the headwaters where they hatched –
those gods of writhing fire and churning water
spawning globular clusters of red dwarf stars –
black dilated eyespots already tracking
movement, already searching for the light.

Witness

After William Carpenter

This morning, I watch my neighbor in her nightgown
swing a nine-iron through the windshield of her husband's
pickup truck, pull out the pitched blade and take
repeated shots at the hood, double cab, oversized bed,
leaving pock-marked dents, as if the family's
gabled home with peaked roof, the neatly trimmed
copse of trees lining the property, even the children's
jungle gym, had been broken off our suburban diorama,
leaving shards of jagged sky to come crashing down
on his most valuable possession. It is a cold day,
and the woman is expelling her breath in heaving clouds
that appear perfectly timed to her swings,
each one followed by the sharp report
of club head against sheet metal. I envy her
energy, since I am still on the porch in my robe
while my neighbor has already totaled
a fifty thousand dollar vehicle. I wonder
what secret she has discovered, what bank account
or email or sales receipt unfolded while he sleeps,
clueless to the damage done. And now the children
are joining in their mother's lively performance, adding
their small pings on chrome rims with toy hammers,
muted cymbal crashes on the headlights. I'd like to
help out myself, go down into my basement
and bring out a sledgehammer for the cause
of her honor. But after all, there's a truck
in my driveway that needs destroying
as much as anyone's. So I simply watch
as the man staggers out the front door,
beer in one hand, ax over shoulder.
He takes a final guzzle before crushing

the can and throwing it into the bed,
cocking the handle down his back
like a cleanup batter in the game of his life.
Then locking his jaw, he takes a full swing
at the front grill which caves in with the amplified
sound of a schoolboy's front teeth being knocked out
by the playground bully, the radiator
dribbling out its oily green blood. Not content,
the crazed man circles his crippled prey,
slamming the axe into every undented square inch.
His wife and kids, having scattered, watch him
from the street, then slowly return
like day laborers from a smoke break,
pick up their tools and, as a wary team,
take up the project of finishing off that truck,
the man and woman working their way
toward each other until, side by side, they are coupled
before their unlucky wreckage. Without intending,
their hands touch. Laughter bursts forth like rain
on an outdoor wedding that should have
never taken place, both spoiling and saving it
at the same time. Then the recoiling —
she slapping him, he grabbing her wrist,
the slipping and falling into the damp grass,
the wrestling and rolling which turns
into kissing, groping, a frenzy of mouths
and legs that have not touched for who knows
how long, taken inside, leaving the children
crying in the yard, and me, embarrassed,
bearing witness to so much love.

Spoils

Torre del Greco, 1944

An average-sized sardonyx shell will yield
one, two, three, diminutive cameos.
How my father came into these hoarfrost ladies

is unknown. Were they lying stone-still on throats, broken
away from their lockets, or pinned as brooches
on blouses heaving to the rhythms of battle? Perhaps

taken from the pocket of an Eisenhower jacket,
breast-up in the nude, red mud of Naples. Murky
as Death's crimson choke. But how I ceded them

to one, two, three wives can now be told: the first
a pendant in lieu of a ring, the second in a post-coital stupor,
the third, ripped from its setting by court order.

Sometimes life curls back on itself in ribbons
of smoking brimstone, as if a master carver were
slicing up Hell with her curved-bladed bulino:

like a poem written years ago turning up
in a pawn shop inside the same envelope
as a loose, rose-colored cameo.

Break
After Kim Addonizio

It feels so good to break a rack of pool balls,
to stand with your legs apart, stroking the cue
between fingers and thumb, aiming at the tight
diamond, then thrusting your pelvis into an explosion
of red and purple and blue – it feels good
to move in on the cue, chalk up your stick,
pound the first ball into the corner pocket
with enough draw to get shape for the next shot.
Then another and another, and you no longer wonder
why some real cool boys skipped school,
how they ended up dead so soon. You can feel them
in your body – the breaking sounds around the room
like the splintering of bones, the firing of Berettas
and Glocks, the jukebox wailing like mothers and fathers.
And now you want to smash every cue in the house,
rip the green felt off each slab of slate,
take a hammer to the balls, a hatchet
to the whorled-grain table legs, douse the place
with gasoline and strike a match, watch the smoke
rise through the bright, silent sky – so high
nothing can reach it. But you're afraid
the cloud would rain down as ash,
feed trees to harvest for more pool halls.
So you stand there knocking in balls
until your stick feels light, innocent.
Then you rack them up again.

American-Amicable Life

> *Erected in 1940, The ALICO Building (for American-Amicable Life InsuranceCompany) was the tallest building west of the Mississippi River, and still stands as the only skyscraper in Waco, Texas.*

Nineteen eighty-one. In an upper room
of the loneliest skyscraper in America,
I sit before the lens of a video camera,
red light blinking, VHS recorder purring.
I am rehearsing my life insurance sales presentation
with two other agents who are pretending
to be husband and wife at the kitchen table
of their multiple-story, mortgaged home.
In a role-play folded into the role-play, neatly
as a commission check inside the secret
pocket of my wallet, I kill off the bread winner
with a runaway bus. Then I ask Mary how
she is going to pay for Will's casket,
the one with magnesium rebar and sealed gaskets
to prevent rust and water from seeping in,
how she is going to keep up the house payments,
send Megan and Benjamin to Baylor as planned
when the future seemed more kind.
The tape lets out a warning squeak,
reaches the end of its loop and ejects.
As the technician reloads a blank,
I look out the twenty-second floor window
at a river, not knowing its name,
not knowing its single-span suspension bridge
was inspiration for the architect to design Brooklyn's,
provide the grist for Hart Crane's vision.
I am not yet a poet, having arrived at the home office
of American-Amicable Life by the road most traveled,
and so I turn back to my canned presentation.
Before I can resume, Mary raises an objection

(which, according to my trainer, like all objections
is only a question in disguise). It's the one
about the high premium for whole life,
how her brother-in-law says they should buy term.
Instead of explaining to Mary the mathematics,
I take her back to the scene of the accident, show her
Will lying on the pavement with no shoes, the blood
oozing from beneath his cuffed pants, spread-collar
shirt blooming like a white napkin soaking up spilled wine.
I make a powerful closing statement then simply stare
out the window again (the rule is *the first one to speak,
loses*). Fog has rolled in, glowing from the neon
ALICO sign above us, condensing and dripping off
the building's shoulders, transparent fingers reaching
for the harp string bridge, the bent, brown arm
of the invisible river below that years later I will learn
is called *El Rio de los Brazos de Dios* –
The River of the Arms of God – embracing all
that is draining off this watershed, in time
taking even this skyscraper to its breast –
every letter, every brick, all the mortar,
the flesh, the water, the rust, this silence.

Dream Ending with a Line By Charles Wright

Three a.m. again. Sitting at my desk,
writing down a dream. From the far ridge
a coyote empties itself into the ravine –
vowels more ancient than distance
between us. I return to bed and search for more
memories beneath my pillow, while the Sun,
crouched somewhere behind the Rockies,
stalks redwoods standing watch over the end
of the continent.   Six a.m. Another dream
insists I rise, get dressed, drive to my appointment
with the trail I walk each day. On my right,
the multimillion-dollar homes that overlook the bay,
on my left, the billions-year-old ocean rising,
reclaiming more ground with each king tide, lapping
cherry doors, beveled glass.
                              I walk fast
and as far as I can in the time I have, keeping watch
behind me, checking for speeding cyclists before I hear
pavement's sibilant resistance, sometimes swearing
I can catch a glimpse of dust rising through the eucalyptus,
the knobby tread and familiar gait of my own approaching
death.
          Soon, it will all reverse – what was right will be left,
the light so gauzy now in morning fog will sharpen
against Mount Tamalpais's edge on my evening commute
home, where I will drift *back to the black beginning.*

Nightshade

My neighbor yells out to be careful opening the back door – a bird
    on the deck not moving, he says, no matter

How close I come to it. I ease out the front and meet him round back
    where a goldfinch is straddling the railing, legs

Dangling, head on its side, neck-down riffling in wind,
    balancing with one wing

On the splintered board, staring through us into the deepest part
    of the garden. What do you think

Is wrong, he asks, pointing to the other two, spread out
    on the patio like angels asleep on concrete clouds,

Beaks open, tongues lolling, eyes blank as clocks without hands.
    I saw this movie, I say, where Earth's electrical charge

Reversed, birds flew into buildings because they couldn't line up
    iron-filled bones with the North Pole. Is this the same

Mystery that causes whales to beach, lemmings to leap off cliffs,
    men to trudge naked out to sea, following the green flash

At sunset? I notice half-chewed berries strewn like a broken rosary,
    hear my mother's beaded voice tell how birds used to die

Eating her nightshade. How her soiled hands scooped up each
    limp, warm bag of feathered sunlight after digging

Their common grave. How she tossed them one by one into the dust-
    flecked air. How their wings spread one last time

On the downside of the parabola they traced. How they flew though dead.

The Gate

To the Golden Gate Bridge

How many sunsets have white hairs of fog
Fallen from the headlands, collected
In the gate's throat like fleece beneath
A sigh of stars? How many torn

Moon-ears, up all night, listening
For the feverish cries of gulls
Sweeping vermilion waves
Through restless shadows?

How much sepia harvested for ink
From octopus, cuttlefish, squid,
Glowing with phosphorescence
Days after they are dead?

And you, golden blade, surrogate stitch
In the continent's deep wound,
Suppurating your stories out to sea,
Stories of limestone, ash, and lava,

How many times have your waters parted, dissolving
Into nothing, then starting up again
In the life of this shorn planet? How many worlds
Collided to flood this valley, slicing

Hills into islands, how many words strung together
Into sonnets beneath your harp strings,
Rising like incense, like a web of vines
Stretching to the mountains where we look for help,

Shrouded in burning clouds, smoking by day,
Glowing by night? How many foghorns
Pressed into the dark wall of sleep,
Like swollen seeds thumbed into humus,

Sprouting to the surface, waiting
For the Sun, that one faithful fire-eye
Blinking through mist, searching for its twin –
The Earth, and all its fullness, turning

Art to life, life to art, the truest
Lovers? How many nights
Has your watery bed swayed
Beneath your broad back? How many days

Has the bay rolled open its scroll of ciphers,
Moon squinting to read page after page
Of surf, all in one glance, before they fade
On a loom of soggy loam, weaving

A landscape more like itself than itself
At each power of magnification, each level
Of imagination, twisting like snowflakes
In an earthquake, ragged white corpuscles

Swimming up the bloodstream to the brain's
Headwaters, where fractals mediate
The amygdala and the Dalai Lama,
Pain of wisdom and ecstasy of speech?

The last cigarette and the iron sea.

1

God, he thinks, how erotic
to pull the cork
from the brown bottle, yellow
wattles on the label, first taste,
when he'd sworn he wouldn't
drink tonight. Tilting the glass
till wine kisses the rim,
then back, he watches legs
curve to the stem, swirling
the red, slowly at first, low
in the bowl, rotating his wrist,
stiffening his arm, spooling
the liquid higher and faster,
thinning pink against
transparent surface. Inhaling
the bouquet of currant,
blackberry, licorice, oak,
he slurps the Syrah, perfectly
balanced with Viognier, the way
a mountain takes spring
snowmelt, chewing water
in its mouth of smooth stones,
spitting out foam with the scent
of life and death rising
above forest's canopy.
He sets down the glass, wine
pooling beneath his tongue
a full minute before swallowing.
Then he tips the bottle to his lips
and drinks because, after all, that's
what he is, isn't he? A drinker
of Viognier, a guzzler
of the world. He gazes

around his North Beach apartment:
empty bottles on recessed shelves,
fox-cornered books, broken
spines and loose pages, speckled
with soot from the furnace, windows
a triptych of bridges: the Bay,
Golden Gate, Richmond-
San Rafael: three strands of lights
strung across water, the last silver
tinsel clinging to Christmas trees
piled in an alley, reflecting
the blinking neon sign from a bar
after last call – business travelers,
drunks, prostitutes: all
gone, except for one homeless figure,
fetal-curled on a sagging couch,
dreaming under water –
air escaping black nostrils –
an unbroken necklace – each bubble
a hollow bead of sooty atmosphere.

2

Imagine no San Francisco bay. Only golden fur
hills shedding rainwater to the river, methodically
emptying an inland sea in the east into the nameless
ocean, beached a long day's journey west. Imagine

cliffs not yet formed that will separate northern tribes
from the peninsula left when Earth lifts herself up,
and the valley cracks and sinks like the center of a cake
taken from the oven too early, before guests

arrive. Instead of a horizon-pinned skyscraper-scape –
mammoths, camels, giant sloth in herds along the riverbank,
a cloud of dust not yet stuck to moist creases on human
faces, in the palm of a hand as it grips a spear

or cradles a baby's head after it passes
from a mother. Imagine ten thousand years
later, sitting in circle, bearing witness to the birth
of the bay, glaciers melting, the ocean rising

enough to reverse the river and flood the valley –
sponges, jellyfish, sea squirt, sharks. Imagine
the surprise of a camouflaged, saber-toothed tiger
circling the first village, flint piercing its side, smoke

curling through the air like the shed skin of a snake.

3

Every morning they climb single file up catenaries,
climb to the top of each tower, where cradles rock
between peninsula and headlands,
the Pacific and *the cool gray city*. Bussed
by salt and fog, the bridge's vermilion lipstick smears
and fades by sublimation directly into a gaseous state.
They apply PMS 173 continually – anchorage, abutments,
bowstrings – paint occasionally dripping and splattering
five hundred feet below onto cement balustrades
at seventy-five miles an hour – a bicyclist's helmet, a tourist's
wrist, splashes of flame, leaving stains on sidewalks,
marks on flesh that turn black and then a permanent gray: proof
they were here, proof they crossed through the Golden Gate.

4

One harness boot is propped
on the bottom rail of the four-
foot fence, under light pole
ninety-seven, the first beyond
the south tower, on the city
side. He points toward Angel
Island, Alcatraz, the piers,
but all that is visible are bare
arms blurring into fog, appearing
as muscular cables
holding up the roadbed,
fading into lead sky
on either side, reminding him
of photographs of the half
constructed bridge, towers standing
in water, ripped arms reaching out
to each other, to each shore, two
crosses fleshed out daily by steel
accretion and streetlamp
glow above him, a color midway
between Moon and setting Sun,
giving the comfort of one naked
light bulb hanging from the frozen family
barn rafter, smell of hay mingled
with horses in the gelid breeze
blowing in from the Pacific, long black
hair lifting off his shoulders, whipping
around his face, cheeks
warming momentarily, before he plants
palms on the top rail, braces, then lifts
damp eyes, turns and retraces his steps.

5

Some fold their laundry the night before,
        place lambskin sweaters chest-down onto the bed,

Cross sleeves behind backs, turn
        ribbed cuffs up, sides in, bend

Cotton bodies into thirds or halves, stack them
        neatly in cedar drawers.

Some line up ponies and riders
        on Polo shirts, underwear devoted

To bottom shelves. Some never touch

Heaps of dirty clothing, leave everything for lovers
        or parents to dispose of....

Some type up notes in Times New Roman:
        poems, diatribes or bizarre encomiums.

Some make videos in drag while drugged
        on popular culture. Some merely hum

As they climb over the railing and stand on the ledge,
        gaze at the piled-up city, waves that suck life

In through the gate, under the bridge, then out to the ocean again.

6
City Angels

Hair the color of wet cement drying,
Younger ones keep their heads
Shaven, hands, necks. They perch on fire
Escapes above the chain-linked dead
End alleys, avoid detection by wearing brownstone
Hooded robes. At dawn they fly off in lines
With pigeons. Old ones take positions
Above numbered avenues in high relief as mimes,
Die without a single feather
Ruffled on wings of admonition. Bound
To architrave friezes of museums and withered
Church steeples, gray mortar pills into sand,
Sifts onto the city like cinnamon,
Like moons spinning on the head of a pin.

7

God spoke to him
through transmissions
of old cars. Waterfalls,
hand saws. Rails
sang like strings
beneath bows of boxcar
cellos. God whispered
from the deep
fried oil at Luke's Café,
taught him how to use a steak
knife, remove a rib
from the waitress, showed him
an escape route through the garden.

In the hospital, there were angels
between the walls. Sobbing
in water pipes, radiators.
They traveled the city in sirens at night,
until his doctors locked them away
behind bars of lithium. Now he stands
on the Golden Gate, listens
to foghorns on the bay, sea lions
billowing up from Pier 39,
prays in unknown tongues, casting
for some lost chord. Only the wind
in the wind. Waves in the waves.

8

On the bridge again:
machine-language-
static-hiss of wind-
quickened strings:
immutable, vertical
sheets of flannel
fog unraveling
seams, dangling
from b&w pixel
sky, four and one
half billion years:
then what happens
to the Golden Gate?
Protons strip off
electron shells, fling
themselves out
of the race to the finish
line of self, lying in non-
locatable space, neuron
neighbors tumbling from
mouths, seeds from stone
fruit, overripe decibels
of fighting lovers above
unidentifiable music
bleeding through a transistor
Delmonico radio resting on
the San Francisco Chronicle
spitting out word salad
trying to get through
to him, trying.

9

Without eldritch cry
Without unified theory
Without threading the camel
through the eye of the needle
Without analog *I*
Without metaphor *me*
creating a perceived operating space
Without detritus
Without sophistry
Without ribs of organized society
Without the privileged moment
Without breakdown of the bicameral mind
Without Elohim explanation
Without Thou
Without Thy
kingdom coming
Without glossolalia
Without scabrous walls
Without flowering rods or staffs –
they fall into the abyss. Without

Zeno's paradox. Without
vibrating string problems. Without
abstractions withdrawn
from particular examples. Without
epileptic aura. Without
symbol or rune. Without
love knots. Without
megrim. Without
absolution, ablution or effusion. Without
consubstantiation. Without
genuflection. Without
genuine reflection. Without

casual confusion syndrome. Without
categorical imperative. Without
within. Without without,
they fall.

10

At the top of the ramp
he waves his plastic card

with electromagnetic strip.
The mechanical arm faithfully bends

at the elbow, then lifts.
The pedestrian warning blares,

but he honks, just to make sure,
before turning right, the only direction he can –

three times. Then left on Columbus,
and North Beach is aswarm with pleasure

seekers: The Purple Onion, The Stinking
Rose, Specs, Cafés Divine and Trieste.

Through the marina with the black diamond
bay off to the right, a lone runner, reflective

tape on hands and legs. Disembodied
bones thrashing the air. Golden spots

beneath the span appear, footlights
to an empty stage before the play begins.

Then the curtain of trees in the park
rises and the bridge appears, claret towers

square, the further one resting
inside the near, both sights on a mile-

long rifle. Flashing gunmetal rain
behind the rain blowing sideways

across the fiery barrel. He speeds through
in the center lane. Is he drifting

or is it the swinging deck
beneath the smoke-filled sky,

above the kneeling waves?

11
Contra Costa

> *... I will make the wilderness a pool of water,*
> *and the dry land springs of water.*
> *... the streams whereof shall make glad the city.*
>   – Isaiah 41:18
>   – Psalms 46:4

High on the hills above Niles Canyon, fog collects
horse silhouettes. An infinite number

of ways to say this gathering of flesh, huddled above
the silver river, cleaving golden hills to the east,

fresh waters flowing west to the brackish south bay,
then north where they meet the sea: a rip

tide opens up the shoreline, page by torn
page, mud sucks at mossed-over beams

of piers swaying with the tides, red-winged
blackbirds singing sunrise: electric

blossoms scattered, thistles. And Mt. Diablo rises,
rises, the Pacific plate continues feeding

the continent through its faults,
spitting out greywacke, chert, and shale

piled up for bobcat and kit fox to stalk a stray
lamb or fawn, an occasional concolor

cougar taking down a full-grown doe
before the Sun warms its riffling coat:

deep beneath the still surface
waters roil inside the machinery

of the estuary, move toward the saline gate,
thickening like muscled hindquarters

hitched to a plow, leaning into its harness
as it passes under the Dumbarton,

the San Mateo, the Bay bridges, past Alcatraz,
Angel Island, San Quentin: the waters

make their final approach, where kite surfers are
flying beneath the bridge, catching the wind, lifting

the chop, spinning before landing
in illegible white caps, beside a steeply-keeled Coast

Guard boat, figures in orange decontamination suits
lined up on the deck, circling an imagined point

of entry, the black diesel smoke drifting toward the fog,
a lugubrious shadow rising, the cutter

completing its final circle, then angling back to perpendicular,
as the waters break through their harness and rush through the gate.

from
Dharma Rain

Vortices

We all eventually stumble into our own story.

Every big bang has an infinite number

Of small bangs struggling to get out.

For our purposes there are no other purposes.

Theoretically the atoms in your left foot came from a star

Different from the one that donated the atoms to your right.

Some theories are full of theorists.

And some holes are full of stories.

Black ones with event horizons big enough to hold

All the lines ever written in the universe.

But that's another story.

Watch your step.

Horse Latitudes

You're driving I-10, somewhere between Las Cruces
and Deming. Feeling grounded. *All Things Considered*
on the radio, stories grazing the brown hills, voices
wet with static, licking at the sparse fence line
of automobile aerials moving west –
something about the legend of The Horse Latitudes,
the roiling vicissitudes of the Cape Horn Ocean
killing the wind, compelling sailors to throw horses
overboard to stay afloat – *They found skeletons, necks
broken, right next to sunken boats.* In the same time frame,
the yellow stripe in the road turns
dark, widens and crosses over into your lane –
a streak of rust, then chestnut for miles. You can see it
beginning to turn again, this time coppery
in smell, and it's damp ahead – definitely
part of your brain says best slow down, says O
God! It's a roan in the road, lying on its side,
tied to the trailer behind a pickup truck,
hindquarters quivering. Quivering
in the blood-soaked arms of two men,
there are children crying, and a woman
is pulling a gun from the cab. As you swing wide,
one of its eyes, an unbroken egg full of white sky,
rolls back and flashes its lightning-red veins.
And in that moment you know everything
in the story is wrong – the ocean, the wind, the killing,
the men, those horses at the bottom of the sea –
they jumped.

A Short History of Baby Incubators

All the World Loves a Baby
– Sign in front of The Baby Incubator sideshow at Coney Island, 1941

They began as *child hatcheries in Berlin*
during the 19th century, but didn't catch on

until Dr. Martin Couney opened up his clinic
as a Coney Island Amusement Park exhibit.

Parents of preemies, given no hope
from hospitals of their day, gave up

their babies to this carnival attraction –
experimental containers set up in a sideshow

where barkers charged a thin dime
to view a pound or two of barely living flesh

through a pane of glass. Assistants dressed up
in white starched uniforms, posed

as doctors and nurses standing at attention
between cubicles, couldn't prevent the struggling

bodies from dying during an outbreak of diarrhea.
Snuggled between the camels and elephants,

the bearded lady and house of mirrors,
nestled in their see-through, straw-lined isolettes,

they passed without mention or funeral,
without gold, frankincense, or myrrh.

Swords, Seed, Gods, & Gold

God came to Abram in heat
of daydream. Said, get thee up

and I will show thee my gash
in the ground, my flowing

River Jordan. Abram woke
his wives, his idols, his pride

of lies, hiding in a cave
named right temporal lobe. Set out

on a journey to the other side
of the fertile scythe with all he owned –

swords, seed, gods, & gold –
seeking the wound that heals

not, the chthonic angel in a slot
machine in the middle of a desert

called religion. Then Abram dreamed
he pulled on God's sweaty handle,

spun his drums until they lined up
as three persons – father, son, & holy

mother. Abram heard a voice
deep in the clatter of God's change

back & forth from one gender
to another. Said, because you bet

on me, you are cursed
with my semen. In your mouth

it will become sermon – a milky
way ever-dying, ever-reborn,

a vision not mine, not yours –
wandering in this desert forever.

When God Moved Out

At first, He visited the children every weekend:
they'd sleep over in the small chapel
He'd taken on the corner across from
The Divine Hand Palm Reading Parlor.

He bathed them in the baptistery beneath
a mural of olive trees on the banks of the River
Jordan, calling down from His study to stop
splashing while He was answering

evening prayers. Later, He'd descend,
tell bedtime stories replete with apocryphal
animal friends, tuck them into sheepskin
pallets He'd made to cushion the pews.

On the Sabbath, of course, God would rest
at the beach in a chaise lounge, call up dolphins
as playmates, periodically check in
with the new girlfriend on His cell phone.

After the divorce was final, He came around
only once or twice a year – Christmas, Easter –
but He was always there in spirit – the weddings,
christenings, funerals – lurking in the corners
of His children's dreams of eternal punishment.

Psalm '66

O '66 Plymouth Valiant! In you will I put my trust.
Your chromed, Barracuda hood ornament leads me.

Your tuck'n roll bucket seats comfort me.
Your 400-horsepower Hemi engine will save me

from being shamed by a Biscayne dragging Main Street.
Though I double-clutch down Red Mountain, I will not fear,

for your disc brakes and Hurst shifter are with me.
Your tubular suspension protects me. Your roll bar

watches over me – a halo of Chrome-Moly black steel.
Your aluminum wheels and Positraction rear end

will carry me from the Midwest to New Mexico.
Even though I cross-country to San Francisco,

I have no need for a motor hotel. In truck stop
parking lots, your double bass exhaust is hushed,

while a waitress prepares a table before me of pork chops,
buttered toast, hash browns, and fried eggs sunny side up.

You anoint my hands with grease. The sweet smell
of gasoline will follow me all the days of my life,

and I will dwell in the pleasures of your back seat forever.

Meet Calvin

Trained from birth in the most fundamental
tenet of fundamentalism – fear –
Calvin lit the other end of his existential candle
by waxing intellectual – no tear
allowed to drizzle over Sundays of frozen emotion
served up by the biggest Father around,
force-fed by a fanatical mother. Religious conversion?
He faked it! – as well as the claim he'd found
the peace that passeth all understanding.
Later, he lied about the call to preach,
abstinence, celibacy, God's blessings –
but not the adrenaline that forbade sleep,
raised his BP, gave him A-fib, PVCs –
not about *what hurt him into poetry.*

He Couldn't Play in Dance Band Because Dancing Was a Sin

But was allowed to take up the trumpet
because it was *the Lord's* instrument,
played by angels to call forth plagues and woes
in the book of Revelation. He practiced for hours
each day on his cousin's beat-up Blessing – private lessons
went so well his father bought him a new Conn Constellation.
The next day, after warming up on "Stardust,"
his trumpet teacher told him that he must
play *the song about a song about love* that night
at the fall concert. After school in the empty band hall,
he closed his eyes, blew through tilted-up bell
the way he'd seen Maynard do –
he envisioned sinners slow-dancing, a darkening moon,
each note calling down a star from the molten sky.

Love Lifted Him Not

He hadn't even known that he was sinking
deep in sin, until his mother told him
not to take the grape juice or the wafers
the deacons would pass down the aisle that night – tapers
reflecting on chrome trays – because Jesus hadn't paid
for *his* sins. Eight years old and on his way
to Hell because he'd never been so bold
as to walk the aisle for Christ, trust the old
rugged cross. *But God still loves you*, said his father.
And so do we, said his mother.
Next day he heard her talking on the telephone:
Calvin's under conviction; please pray for his soul.
Yes, he thought, *I do need help from above,*
lest I drown in these angry waves of love.

Dharma Rain

In the summer of 2008, when wildfire descended on Tassajara Zen Center, the oldest Zen monastery outside Asia, the Forest Service evacuated all residents. Five monks turned back and met the fire, saving Tassajara.
— Adapted from *Fire Monks: Zen Mind Meets Wildfire at the Gates of Tassajara*

It was Dharma Rain
        met you, Dharma Rain
from *granite wine*

        pumped from the creek
through PVC pipe
        soaking wooden buildings,

dirt, stone, skin –
        sprinklers the sound
of sustained violins –

        strings creating their own
sultry atmosphere –
        your fiery, brass choir

waiting for director's baton
        to cue you in. It was the Fire
Monk Jazz Quintet

        rearranged the score,
re-harmonized minor-chord flame-songs –
        Jump, Jive, An' Wailin'

fire-hose saxophones
        swingin' with your drivin'
hot-rock rhythms

    and log-rollin' bass notes,
cascading down into the smoke-
    filled Tassajara gulch,

the whole valley smelling
   like the world's original singe –
you, up on the ridge,

   ripping off red blouses
from manzanitas and madrones,
   becoming more aroused

with each naked limb, each torso
   exposed in firelight.
You crowned them one by one,

   but couldn't penetrate
the V-shaped ravine, though you tried
   like a groom on his wedding night

but in the end, more out of duty
   than desire, you stumbled drunk
into the bed

   of the garden, soft
glow buried in her
   loam, her mist.

    • • •

Conceived of flash
   between Earth and sky,
I smoldered three days

   beneath dust. Born hungry
for live oak, sycamore,
   maple – compelled to carve

paths through chaparral,
    maroon-barked manzanita,
chamise, ceanothus, yucca,

    to enlighten all flesh
in my oven mouth —
    one breath

to translate a trillion tree lines,
    a billion pages of bay laurel
into fire beetles and whispering bells.

    O Tassajara,
when your lanterns were lit
    along the Engawa

surrounding your zendo
    this morning, I saw you —
the frost of your skin, your body,

    your vulnerable ground,
fire-monk boots making little Buddha-shapes
    in the wet dirt.

I saw your treetops aligned
    like piano keys,
each taut string

    tied to nothingness, waiting
for my vermilion finger
    -nailed touch.

Then I turned
    to the moist commerce
of your temple gate and yurts,

sheds and chemicals,
pine rooms and cabins,
birdhouse and pool,

your schist Buddha,
eyes brushed closed,
buried in the bocce ball court,

calling down my parched tongues
to lap your Dharma Rain, your granite wine,
to suckle the icicle of you.

Spirit

After Campbell McGrath

We construct it from water and motion and breath,
        smoke, tremors, tongues
        of fire, desire to live between
growing distances of the stars.

It is, for all its freedom and aspiration,
        an artifact of human agency –
        the universe become conscious,
poured into cracked urns of flesh.

Its insistent voice mirrored by a hungry ear,
        like the lesser light that rules the night
        reflecting the Ancient of Days. Old
as the odor of resin-soaked wood on the pyre,

dancing to blood-orange flames,
        fashioned from the atmosphere,
        dark matter, energy, air,
shaped and assembled deed by deed,

and finished with feathers of ice.
        We build it on a loom that turns
        straw thoughts into golden bullion,
then lock it in its chest and hope it can save us.

Recycling

I am wheeling the recycling bin
down the driveway, the steep
pot-holed driveway, eighteen percent
grade – impossible for trucks
to negotiate up through
freighted foliage to our house.
I am thinking about the plastic
Arrowhead water bottles, broken down
cardboard boxes, Ball Mason jars
with a faint grape odor
I am sending out into the world
after having consumed their contents –
I am wondering where they will go,
if I will see them again, and if I would
recognize them in an altered form
or universe.   I am pondering the day
wood pulp in the cardboard was conceived
from a single photon of sunlight striking
one green leaf of perhaps the great-
great-grandmother of this eucalyptus tree
or that balsam fir. And I am amazed at the thought
of breathing in molecules of air,
exhaled from plants, as well as from people
dead for years – Darwin, Shakespeare,
Whitman, Crane – swirling in my lungs,
their embered words unreadable
heat signatures, along with the last breath
sucked from the chest of some rapist
on death row, a thief
hanging on a cross by nails
fashioned from iron smelted in a star
gone nova over five billion years ago –

the same metal hammering through my veins,
feverishly trying to get more
oxygen to my legs, as I walk
back up the crumbling asphalt,
loose gravel anting oceanward – mother
ocean stretching up as tall as she can with every wave
for a glimpse of her prodigal children returning home.

To the Fog

And then you wake up one morning to the fog
surrounding your house like a heaven,
like the first time you drank a whole bottle
of white wine alone. You get dressed
for the path you walk each day.
You look to the horizon, the shouting
Sun now more like Moon's soft hum, one muted tone
behind sky's veil. You notice the lichen-
covered stones greeting each step, the geometry
of downed limbs scratching at low tide,
the snowy egret you surprise, plumed head
turned on its side, sweeping the mudflats, improvising
a way to catch breakfast in suffused light—
all of this and more, normally hidden in plain sight.
But an orchestra's warming up behind the curtain:
commuters leaning on shrill horns, distant
sirens rising, the engines of this world
revving up their clear intent to perform
something short of a miracle. O fog of morning,
hover in the hollows of this day,
linger in low places, to rise up again
when we need not more, but less.

from
The Thing Itself

Neighbors at 2 a.m.

They're fighting again. Shouting and throwing
clothes off their balcony, several stories
above us – billowing silk blouses, distressed
jeans – flailing half-human forms plunging
toward cool sod like suicides. One by one,
lights are coming on in the courtyard of the complex.
A humid night, gray-green fog has gathered
in damp St. Augustine, like the angel of death
in Cecil B. DeMille's *The Ten Commandments*.
Shouldn't we smear blood on our doorposts,
our lintels? Blood – isn't that what *they* are after,
turning themselves inside out, drowning
each other in the rapids of their hearts,
getting swept over the falls, swearing a final oath
in Oblivion's bittersweet name? Shouldn't we all
gather at the river, tread its bright banks,
find a sacred spot where laurels exhale their long, unison breath –
every leaf a tongue, every branch a choir
canting its last overture? Don't we need to
sit zazen in the midst of gnarled trunks,
offer confessions? Listen – now the sound
of furniture breaking on the rocks below,
a surfeit of hate shaking our foundation –
flecks of spackle sifting through
the tired light of our own closets,
like sequins falling from a wedding gown.

Morning Ritual

In the mirror, I inventory spots and lumps
on my mostly denuded body, assessing

any change in color or size. I visualize
eight million years of hair loss, ancestors

once semi-aquatic later suffering heat stroke –
perhaps irritating parasitic beginnings

of malaria or Lyme disease – as they moved
out of the African savanna.

My triple-bladed razor excises
traces of hirsute lineage from my space-time face.

Safely tucked beneath hair and bone,
mitochondria in my brain rehearse

their workday full of meetings to decide
which cells live, which die, what diseases

will be revealed on my epidermis before
our star swells to the size of Mars's orbit,

before blood and bumps boil away –
before tonight's bottle of Beaujolais.

By Any Other Name
August 2006

They voted Pluto off the list of planets,
one less note in the music of the spheres.
News of this reaches me too late to show up

for the debate and argue for snowball dwarfs,
diminution, and eccentric orbs
cutting through the plane of Neptune – instead

I will write this missive and read the annual
reports, which I predict will change as bodies
wobble their way in and out of favor. Also,

I will listen to the sound of my Apple
laptop instead of my manual Remington
cutting into twenty-pound paper, ink

filling in depressions and gashes
on scrolled pages. What isn't history?
Or for that matter, this story of changing

names and places, written in fading script – yes
there are nights you could read by the light
cast upon Pluto by its full moon, Styx.

Safeway

I love my grocery store. I love to roam
its aisles – Keebler Elves, the Jolly Green Giant

shuffling for position with jellied Spam,
frozen pizza plastered with pepperoni

discs ready to fly down my throat, hover
in my stomach, disembark its fat

little passengers to march straight to my heart.
The floral department's sign reads *Poetry*

in Bloom above papery black edges of roses red
and violets blue. You can have your Trader Joe's,

your Whole Foods, your non-GMO, gluten-free,
organic-only Good Earth. I want a real grocery store

with hormones in the beef, pharmacy attached, pain
killers within arm's reach of a packaged heart attack.

My Safeway makes me feel safe. Come the apocalypse,
I'll be trapped inside, popping Oxycodone, singing

in the singularity techies say is coming, thawing out a T-bone
on a Weber grill, drinking a ten dollar bottle of pinot,

staring out the window for signs of life –
death. Pretty much doing what I do now at home.

I never wanted to be a poet

before we moved into that converted gas station
on the outskirts of Deming, where dust storms gave up
their ghosts to the shapes of cars and trucks –
one minute nothing out our window but brown
canvas, the next a traveler drawn in
beside lifeless pumps, staggering toward our door,
screams and slaps cutting through sand's static
as the office sign swung against stucco façade.
But something else, one of us said, did you hear
sounds of a trapped animal crying
to open up goddammit and give them some gas
to get out of this hellhole? Once,
when you were naked and alone, standing
in the grease pit now our living room,
a man walked in on you because I'd failed
to lock the door. Later, when you told me the story,
you yelled for the first time in our young marriage
and I joined the chorus, howling the song of every lobo
that longs to be somewhere else. That's when I knew
I had to break loose from the pack
into the open spaces of the poem.

Shiprock

Tsé Bit A'í

Cutting your way through dust storms, sand
Waves over your prow, settles on foils of stone,
Washes down ribs of your hull to crystal sea.

> *The Navajos say you sailed from the north,*
> *A great bird saving their people from the flood,*
> *Crashing into the desert, burying all*
> *But your wings and tail: sole cremains of salvation.*

What is it that makes a man or woman
Set out on foot for you? Your jagged masts that reach
For gibbous moon? Ancient lens of atmosphere?

> *The old ones still believe the blood*
> *Will return to petrified feathers,*
> *Carry them away when the flood returns.*

Grasses and sedges with no names, abandoned
Frames of cars and trucks, valley of dried bones
That will never rest, never rise again?

> *Shiprock! Cry out from beneath the desert;*
> *Call your brothers and sisters from the flood.*

The overwhelming flood of sand
Is all that will mark their graves.

> *Sand enough to stem the flood.*

New Mexico Sighting
Melanistic Canis latrans

A wild dog, we thought, at least partly
fed by Navajos – erect body shining
like a seal's, soaked with the afternoon
Sun – all we could make of your gaze
at two hundred yards. But when you turned,
silhouetting your muzzle, loping into the desert,
tail swaying like a juniper bush,
as much at home among the sage as sage
itself, we knew you were not tracking
hogans painted on the horizon. Descending
the plutonic spine that percolated up through
this plateau twenty-six million years ago, we lost
sight of you, but still whispered as if you were
trickster god we didn't want to wake, dream
we didn't want to leave, longing for one
more glimpse, somehow to confirm
your presence, your mystery – and ours.

Dear Frogs of Pinckneyville, Illinois

Forgive me for all the times I forced you
into Welch's Grape Jelly jars filled with cotton balls
soaked with ether from my father's starter fluid can

he used to fire up dead diesel engines
on frozen December mornings. I am truly sorry
for not throwing you higher. Please know I tried to

place you into orbit like Belka and Strelka,
first Russian dogs to trick gravity and return
alive, but my nine-year-old arm wasn't strong enough

to launch you over the peak of the barn's roof
crumbling into itself in the vacant lot next door.
I tried again and again as you tumbled behind glass

like green-clad daredevils in clothes dryers.
Naturally, I performed post-mortems, the point
of my mother's sewing scissors fitting perfectly

into openings seemingly created for entry. I squeezed
your wart-rough sides and lifted your white bellies
to avoid organs when I opened you up. You voiced no objections

when I showed the neighbor kids your digestive systems,
the contents of your stomachs, your kinked intestines –
totally in the interest of science. Like the other animals

slain so humans could travel safely to the Moon.
I am sorry for them, too. But not as much
as for treating you as if you were created for us

to experiment upon in order to protect those mothers' babies
who grew up to be astronauts. As if the empty womb
of space wasn't holy. As if you were not.

Slow Dancing

In high school, my mother forbade me to play
in Dance Band because swinging hips to music
was a sin. So instead, I bugled at funerals

conducted by the Veterans of Foreign Wars,
although at Green Lawn Cemetery, after twenty-one
gun salutes, I witnessed mourning bodies

swaying to ancient rhythms, holding partners close, howling
like lovers in need of release, as my trumpet sounded
"Taps" – the title said to come from the Dutch *taptoe*,

meaning *close the beer taps and send the troops home.*
Signed by my mother, a permission slip on file
in the principal's office allowed the VFW

post commander to spring me from class an hour or two
before the service began. Al would call our house the night before –
I'd tell Mom I'd be burying the dead the next afternoon.

The VFW Hall was really a bar with a jukebox and pool table.
Al and his buddies played for money, drank beer, and swapped yarns
from two world wars, while drunks dusted the dance floor

to Benny Goodman's licorice stick. As uniformed men loaded
rifles and flags into the van, I got to practice shots on the green felt.
Driving out to the cemetery, Al shook out a Sen-Sen into my palm,

reminded me not to tell Mom what went on down at the VFW Hall.
It's okay, I wasn't playing the music people were dancing to,
I told him, making my transgressions venial.

A problem would only have arisen had she known
the mortal sins of mourners slow dancing to my horn.

A Small Pebble

> *"Calculus," the branch of mathematics originally based on the summation of infinitesimal differences, is translated from the Latin as "a small pebble," like those used in an abacus.*

A redheaded young man in uniform
stares at a laminate menu, nervous
waitress waiting for him to decide between
coffee and tea. A calculus problem,

the solution to which will let him sit
in the corner booth until her shift ends.
Eyeing a four top by the door ready
for their check, she senses a smaller tip
with each metronomic tock of fate's clock.

Coffee, black, he says. She tilts her Pyrex
pot toward his empty cup, reaches for the
bill of fare. He touches her hand, blurts out
a bold question. *Why?* she asks, withdrawing
her glass globe of burnt elixir. *Because...*
and he whispers something unexpected.

Now it's her turn to decide. And although
I'll not meet her for years, I have
much at stake in her decision –
will she agree to a first date, rushed
marriage a month after Pearl Harbor,
before he ships out for North Africa?

And when I tell you they are my parents,
you'll likely guess what she did, but not how
she turned away from the table, untied
her apron, chucked it at her boss
along with her carbon-papered order pad,
walked past waiting customers to the porch,

picked a pebble from between two rough boards,
tossed it up, let it fall into her callused hand
like a loaded die, and threw it as hard
as she could at the newly paved asphalt,
where it skipped a few times before it stuck
in the hot, dark tar, sank, and disappeared,
becoming one with the road forever.

All roads

lead back to my mother swimming in black
humus, gumming the roots of the lupine

like an orchestra behind the curtain
tuning to concert A, the conductor

tapping her baton on the music stand,
waiting for bows across strings to settle

the score, free flags from seeds of notes rising
on the gorged page to wave in space above

staff lines – the concave mirror of the bell
of my trumpet, nickel-plated muzzle

on my lips, night after night, translucent
bullets of saliva drip like white wine

from a goblet, served on a tray of thorns
stabbing both hands, & the stems of my arms

where the pain swerves to the shoulder
of the road that leads back to my mother.

The Thing Itself (A Cento)

You know how hard it is sometimes just to walk on the streets
Downtown, how everything enters you –
Iron straight from the forge, fierce with tiny agitation,
Rain ringing like teeth in the beggar's tin,
Like a sinking ship drowning its lights,
Chalk beds   trilobites   giant ferns
Whirr. The invisible sponsored again by white
Isotopes, pockets, dragonflies, bread:
There is no dictionary for this gathering.
You might think you were Noah
Failing to arrange a taxonomy of allergic substances.
Our lives are like birds' lives, flying around, blown away,
Or some far horn repeating over water –
Do we simply join our arcs
The way a seed is pressed into a hole?
Don't ask me any questions, I've seen how things
Blink-quick, or quicker still,
Tracked under the brown fog of a winter dawn,
Follow the light, the twist and drop of blackbirds from the tree.

Everything: New Poems

Cento with a Few Old Books Thrown In

First line has to make your brain race that's how Frank O'Hara does it.
Like an ice-bound tornado,

almost all the words we've said to one another are gone.
What is the statute of limitations?

We were going toward nothing all along.
It's not the absence in the presence but the presence in the absence.

It is difficult to describe what we felt after we had paid the admission.
Seems to me I have & am thankful for the complete sets of limericks
       and sensory topics.

And there's plenty to be unhappy about
as sunlight slants down on another late afternoon.

I want a different dictionary. (And a different country.)
The poem offers a multiple fold for carrying.

I returned your books of poetry to the store.
There they were. Short, spread out. Deathless and without design.

And yet it didn't seem to matter at all.

Refusal with Broken Wheel

Shirts slung over shoulder, hangers sagging – gravity's
persistent hand – trudging up
floating concrete steps, gaps wide enough to swallow feet
misplaced, freighting belongings –
one more motel room – threadbare boxes, books, mementos
alone make for multiple
crossings of the parking lot, sallow light – sodium
bulbs perched on poles, sentinels
like the ones that watched over your high school stadium
Friday nights while bulked-up boys
slammed each other to the ground & green-epauletted
marching bands rocked Sousaphones –
tunes your parents slow danced to, rearranged now – upbeat
tempo & trumpets & more
drums than anyone knew this universe held – seems like
forever you've been pulling
luggage or a luggage-shaped loneliness, one broken
wheel refusing to turn, till
you cradle the meshed case, mount the final flight, cardkey
door, cross over the threshold
to rented bed – Tumi zipper refusing to yield,
teeth gritted, growling *enough*.

Sheltering in Place with Steely Dan

I discover more of God in my Hoka running shoes
than in the words of Hosea.
Vultures perched on my neighbor's gutter
look at me with disgust. "All this time,"
they say, "and not a single poem
in *Poetry Magazine*." "Only a fool would say that,"
croons Donald Fagen. I turn up the volume to breaking
news on MSNBC. Another shooting and why
doesn't someone wave an AK-15
at those red-faced buzzards pretending to be eagles
while devouring a half-million people. I curse again
and again, placing an order with Amazon
for a Whole Foods pickup. It really sucks
when I can't find a delivery time
in my zip code. For months I've been running low
on mental health. My therapist says it's endemic
among groups that believe salvation
is predestined. She says we need disease to grow,
the way a dead fish feeds a kernel of corn
dropped into a hole. I learned that
in grade school studying American Indians –
their contribution to our great nation. "Thanks
for all the fish" were the last words whistled by dolphins
in *The Hitchhiker's Guide to the Galaxy*.
I want a better way to say goodbye
than "Drink your big black cow and get outta here."
But I have to run. God is waiting.

My Father Draws His Colt .45 for the Final Time
New York Harbor, 3 January 1946

A day like today – above the skyline, curves of clouds,
turquoise-veined water necklacing Queen Mary's prow
riding low beneath the weight of troops on deck – eleven thousand

returning from WWII. My father must have seen – piercing the mist –
the Empire State Building, or perhaps he leaned away from edifices,
faced the blank bank when he drew his pearl-handled .45 –

my mother's pic laminated beneath the grip – then released its weight
to the depths. He must have felt freedom grafted to regret,
the way cadaver skin might save a burn victim. When I was seven,

he told me the story of throwing overboard every weapon –
German Luger, M-1 Garand rifle, the one that earned him
the Combat Infantryman Badge for hand-to-hand –

that decoration and more – Purple Heart, a presidential citation, six bronze
stars – even swastikas, SS insignias, Nazi officer bars – I threw them all
into his casket before we lowered him a half-century later.

Some days like today, mammatus clouds hang down, suckle the ground,
feeding Earth great volumes of darkness and light, choral shells
reflecting sound – far cries across water – cries of freedom, cries of regret.

Upright

My mother played piano by ear –
childhood brush arbor revival meeting
hymns. Right hand picked out the tunes, left stretched and flattened
to a blue-veined sting ray that darted from the depths of her
made-up bass line to feed on midrange chords.

Sharps, flats, naturals, accidentals – she hit them all
without knowing notes or white keys from black –
just what sounded right to her ear. Good thing
she didn't need practice. A piano – so fashionable
on display in a prominent living room spot
during post-war years of American Camelot –
never graced one of our bare-walled rentals.

I only heard her play in the empty sanctuary
before church services until I was in college –
my father bought her a house wholly
furnished with the belongings of a man
whose wife ran off with some preacher or deacon –
I can't remember which.
                         I'm sure the couple were good
parents, wanting the best for their children,
unlike my mother's father who forbade her to compete
in the state piano contest because he saw no sense in girls
attending high school when they should be tending
to men. This husband walked away from everything –

Christmas tree, Barbie dolls, GI Joes, an early American
china cabinet full of real china and silver, the dining room
table where his kids shook cereal from a box
covered with a picture of Roger Maris holding a bat,
the bed where, at least twice, his seed swam
across the void between him and his wife.

And in the living room, a blond Baldwin upright
piano – perhaps a birthday gift for his daughter,
hoping she might be discovered on Ted Mack's
Amateur Hour, or make it onto Arthur Godfrey's
Talent Scouts. The first time I walked into that house
my mother was seated on the wooden bench –
back to the front door, left hand rag-timing
up and down the keyboard from bass notes to chords.

She was wearing her blue housecoat,
but I felt I was intruding the same way
as when I walked in on her nakedness
as a child. I had never seen her body
so alone, yet so immersed in the universe –
a rogue wave curling into itself, still so upright.

Break Room

Walls, once milk-white, now scalded from the flame
of years, a broken black line from folding chairs
leaned back, scuffing paint. You can tell
full-timers – propped-up feet, the way they sit
on brocade cushions brought from home,
while temps eat erect, not knowing how
to spot employees from Loss Prevention.
Half a vending machine sandwich drying
in a plastic triangle – someone called back to the sales floor.
Lettuce too green to be real droops over
stale crusts like a clock in a Dalí painting.
On the big screen, Ken and Barbie
read the news from a teleprompter, eyes
scanning tired faces. A winter storm
in Midwestern cities everyone is happy
they don't live in. Volume too low to make out
words, but no one cares. Except for the iPhones,
you might think this a meditation class,
the way everyone seems mindful
of only the present moment. Each act a ritual
counting of minutes before clocking back in.
Someone lifts a Styrofoam cup, drains the last
caffeinated drop. Another flips back a shirt cuff,
checks a watch. Without acknowledgment,
the room registers the gathering of scraps,
snaps of Tupperware lids, open fridge
chill, final disposition of trash. Then the moaning
hinge of the break room door, sigh
of pneumatic stopper – the latch bolt's click.

Intermission

> *Infinity is just time on an ego trip.*
>   – Lily Tomlin

> *Ego is just time on an infinity trip.*
>   – Fred Alan Wolf

And then we come to the end
of another pornographic year

crawling across the nude stage
feeling for unexploded ordnance,

audience discussing Tarkovsky
movies – precisely what angles

are needed to shoot immediate
futures. In bed after the show

comparing stories – true
history of Western civilization.

Black Suns
Jutland, Denmark

– starlings sweep across the sky
                         as if a magnetized wand were
herding black sand toward
                         Wooly Willy's giant face, or Hair-do
Harriet's bald head, a whim
                         of some larger-than-life child
residing in the heavens –
                         pixelating flocks shape-shifting
above Tonder and Ribe
                         every spring sunset evening
then leaving for breeding ranges,
                         mid-April. Scientists have written
code for the inexplicable living
                         clouds. It's simple, they say –
begin with random moving
                         dots in every direction,
simple rules:
                         move at the same speed,
stay close to your neighbor,
                         avoid danger. A poet
in a crowd of strangers,
                         walking downtown, stares at chaos,
he plies the laws…
                         the universe begins

to make sense. He thinks

                                        again about the black

suns of her eyes,

                                        prominences arcing

toward his, radiating flecks

                                        and streaks

dilating to a storm –

                                        he understands

nothing. He is only a child

                                        searching for a magic wand.

Dearborn Street

Printer's Row, Chicago

I stumbled onto a quivering mound of pigeons,
feathered nacre, iridescent, fluffed,

holding at bay the grave cold
beneath a sky with neither stars nor snow,

nor anything not fashioned from steel, concrete, glass.
I thought on these birds gathered, this dirt-white ground,

how my life was above in a 36th floor apartment, estranged –
my wife living in the back bedroom

building ceiling-high, Lego models of skyscrapers –
John Hancock, Sears Tower, 311 South Wacker –

tallest building in the world with only an address
for its name. Days, I didn't see her. Nights, I waited in vain

listening for Lake Michigan's wet sand confessions.
I peered through my window into nothingness some saw as water.

Not even the Moon reflected at that angle. And if ever an angel
aimed moonlight toward me, it passed through

my glass-top desk capturing nothing – a nothing that had everything
to do with us. My companions were a Korg electric piano,

king-size bed, and a see-through desk, feeding me
enough to stay alive – all I owned in that living room,

closets emptied, suitcases filled, ready for flight. So ready,
had my phone rung – someone from my past offering a plane ticket,

I would have given away piano, desk, bed,
ridden the El to O'Hare by 6 a.m. – which, in the end, I did.

But on that night, I wanted to stay forever on Dearborn,
spellbound by that pile of pigeons, huddled together,
burbling their brief triumph.

The Past

When the past comes to you through the cat door
as a one-eyed raccoon, scrounging for food at 4 a.m. –

you lie awake in bed listening to claws whisper
along the kitchen floor – *Why did she? Why didn't you?* –

don't feed it or chase it with your ex's broom.
And don't ever attempt to embrace the beast –

remember how the past smells, carries disease,
leaves muddy tracks – & those claws & teeth

have dug up moldy roots & grubs & who knows what out back.
Leave it be. It will depart of its own accord if you pay no mind –

tomorrow, buy yourself a *present* – a new door –
you haven't had a cat in years, not since you let it out

at dawn in 2010 & a coyote whisked it across
the rainbow bridge – listen! The cat flap again,

now silence –
slip out of bed, inch downstairs, get on your knees –

sponge, squeeze, sponge, squeeze –
until the smudged tiles begin to shine.

Room Therapy

A room should feel like the fort you built as a child – blankets
and sheets draped over brocade chairs, cushions scattered, secrets –

at night, walls should sing to the broken
and the jubilant should hear the Mormon Tabernacle Choir.

If on the 37th floor, it should have a water view, green-flash sunsets –
if lower, a conifer out the window with juncos fledging.

There should be a desk, large enough for an organized mess –
books and books and drafts of future prize-winning poems,

signs of love-making on the floor, the divan – pillows
creased and marinated, aromas of wine and exertion.

There will be space enough for dogs and children –
but no toys, no dogs, no children. Only a window ledge

wide enough to protect the cat from high-rise syndrome,
wide enough to stand upon when your lover is gone.

Desktop Cento

It's midnight and a light rain falls.
The pines rub their great noise
Toward the place of dreaming and fractions.

If you want to live in the country, you have to understand the power
Of the inky, dismal, and unprofitable research of a recent leave.
A stranger sleeps next to me, a stone beside another stone.

Have you never felt like this, everyone you know
Asking, as usual, for love, for more anyway than you have?
I have come to hate myself, which keeps us both alive.

Tonight, the reigning notes are lost octaves hung out to dry.
There's no telling what the morning will bring
But the absence of stars.

Everything

Tonight, because all matter is dissolving, you & I
are being gradually undressed by the universe –

silk & wool molecules mingling with cells
rising from skin like souls, drifting

into flames, ascending chimney's brick
& mortar atomic particles greeting our neighbor's

barbecue dinner likewise rising toward galaxy's arms,
alongside syringol from the grill it was smoked on –

while my shirt & your skirt fall to the floor.

Climbing stairs to our bedroom, we take care
lest the flood lights break, weakened by an electron choir

escaping into the back yard, joining a rapture of trees
also disappearing. Someday, this house

will be cleansed of all dust & detritus. Mantel
pictures only silhouettes on Kodachrome surfaces,

tombstones, damp caskets beneath, flora feeding
in our guts, while our bodies feast on each other in bed –

everything yes everything now gathered to us is leaving.

Erasure Ending in the Sound of Sweet Nothing

Spinning forty thousand miles a minute around Earth's axis,
over a million miles a minute around our Sun –
heron, mice, pine tree – there should be more explanation.
Match, priest, university – I am forever listening.

Certain prayers are too deep for speech.
The colors were just a parable.
I've been writing in this place
you've always dreamt of –
dark shapes, sharp angles
persist, falter.

I listen inside the lock of my brain for scrape of Earth's key,
form discovered as some sort of imperative –
deflated with prayer, my compass points everywhere.

Mirror.
Window.
Sliding panel.
Gray eye.
Another picture.
A single sword.

All that glitters isn't a bar in Chicago.
Every story has a question about a sound of far-off thunder.

Sun, God, love – I crave them all,
but nothing until the camera pans a landscape
and a river comes along with fish like words
out of God's shallows.

Because desire burns in bright moonlight,
the loudest sigh of all.

All else is illusion – pear, winter, being
human has fastened my body to flesh, sunlight
to eucalyptus, shadow to a wagon rut – something alien,
something alone.

Acknowledgments

My gratitude to the following presses, anthologies, and journals, where these poems first appeared, sometimes in previous versions and/or with different titles:

Chapbooks and Full-Length Collections:

San Gabriel Valley Literary Festival judges for poems taken from *Altar Call*, one of four winning chapbooks in the 2013 anthology *Diesel*.

Southeast Missouri State University Press for poems taken from *If They Have Ears to Hear*, winner of the 2012 Copperdome Chapbook Award.

WordTech Communications (*CW Books*, 2016) for poems taken from *In This Room*.

Saint Julian Press (2016) for poems taken from *Dharma Rain*.

Longship Press (2020) for poems taken from *The Thing Itself*.

Anthologies and Journals:

Blood on the Floor: How Writers Survive Rejection (Cairn Press, 2014) for "Suspects."

Pandemic Puzzle Poems (Blue Light Press) for "Sheltering in Place with Steely Dan."

Poets & Artists for "My Father Draws His Colt .45 for the Final Time." This poem is also included in the Lunar Codex Project that sent digital copies on a rocket ship to the Moon.

Great River Review for "Upright."
Zocalo Public Square for "Break Room."
Puerto del Sol for "Black Suns."
Free State Review for "Dearborn Street."
The Sun for "Everything."

My deepest gratitude to Michael Waters for his mentorship, friendship, and poems which have guided me in my writing life for most of two decades, as well as to Tayve Neese, Elizabeth Oxley, and Jim Benton, whose poems and comments have made my poems stronger and whose friendships have sustained me. My gratitude to Diane Frank of Blue Light Press for her acceptance and support of this book, and to Erik Ievins and Elizabeth Oxley for their superb proofreading. Thank you Joan Baranow and David Groff for your close reading of my work over the years. And thank you Melanie Gendron for all of the final edits to bring this collection to completion. Finally, thank you to my students – you have been my teachers as well.

Notes

"Meet Calvin"

The peace that passeth all understanding is from the New Testament letter by Saint Paul to the Philippians found in chapter 4, verse 7: *And the peace of God, which passeth all understanding, shall keep your hearts and minds through Christ Jesus.*

The abbreviations "BP," "A-fib," and "PVCs" refer to blood pressure, atrial fibrillation, and pre-ventricular contractions respectively.

What hurt him into poetry is from W. H. Auden's poem "In Memory of W. B. Yeats": *Mad Ireland hurt you into poetry.*

"He Couldn't Play in Dance Band Because Dancing Was a Sin"

"Blessing" refers to the E. K. Blessing Company of Saint Louis that has made trumpets since 1906.

The Song about a song about love refers to "Stardust," the first major song ever written about a song that didn't exist, composed by Hoagy Carmichael in 1927.

"Maynard" refers to Maynard Ferguson, the Canadian jazz musician and bandleader who had the habit of lifting the bell of his trumpet above horizontal as he played.

"Love Lifted Him Not"

The title is taken from the hymn "Love Lifted Me" containing the first-stanza lyrics: *I was sinking deep in sin, far from the peaceful shore, / very deeply stained within, sinking to rise no more. / Then the master of the sea heard my despairing cry, / from the waters lifted me, now safe am I.*

"Dharma Rain"

"Dharma Rain" was the name monks at Tassajara Zen Center gave to the sprinkler system they fashioned from PVC pipe that carries water from the creek to the roofs of the main buildings to keep them damp when threatened by wildfires. When the system ran for several weeks prior to the confluence of wildfires that threatened Tassajara in the summer of 2008, it created its own climate in the valley that helped to deplete the fire of its energy as it descended upon the grounds of the monastery.

"The Thing Itself (A Cento)"

The title and lines are taken from poems by Wallace Stevens, Kim Addonizio, Greg Keith, Li-Young Lee, Vicente Huidobro, Amy Gerstler, Jorie Graham, Susan Wheeler, Rachel Blau DuPlessis, Matthew Niblock, Chris Gordon, Charles Wright, Donald Justice, Gabriel Spera, Federico Garcia Lorca, Matt Rader, T. S. Elliot, and Jim Nason.

"Cento with a Few Old Books Thrown In" borrows line fragments and entire lines from poems in the 2004 edition of *Best American Poetry*, edited by David Lehman, written by the following poets: Anne Carson, Will Alexander, Rae Armantrout, Alan Bernheimer, Mary Jo Bang, Charles Bernstein, Billy Collins, Michael Costello, Michael Davidson, Linh Dinh, Rachel Blau DuPlessis, Arielle Greenberg, and Carla Harryman.

"Desktop Cento" borrows lines from books found on my desk:

> Line 1 from Dorianne Laux's "Ghosts" (*Awake*, Carnegie Mellon, 1990)
> Line 1 from Dorianne Laux's "The Life of Trees" (*Facts About the Moon*, Norton, 2006)
> Line 11 from Dorianne Laux's "Staff Sgt. Metz" (*The Book of Men*, Norton, 2006)

Line 1 from Gerald Stern's "The Power of Maples"
(*Lucky Life*, Carnegie Mellon, 1995)
Line 1 from Srikanth Reddy's "I" (*Underworld Lit*, Wave, 2020)
Lines 1-2 from Mihaela Moscaliuc's "Found Poem" (*Cemetery Ink*, Pittsburgh, 2021)
Lines 10b-11 from Larry Levis's "The Two Trees" (*Elegy*, Pittsburgh, 1997)
Line 7 from Kim Addonizio's "The Singing" (*Tell Me*, BOA, 2000)
Lines 14 & 26 from Michael Waters's "Self-Portrait with Doll" (*Caw*, BOA, 2020)
Lines 9a & 10 from Amy Gerstler's "The Slightly Perverse World of Music" (*Ghost Girl*)
Line 1 from Matthew Dickman's "Gas Station" (*Mayakovsky's Revolver*, Norton, 2012)
Line 2 (reworked) from Matthew Dickman's "Gas Station" (*All-American Poem, APR*, 2008)

"Erasure Ending in the Sound of Sweet Nothing" is a cross-out of several poems from multiple volumes of *Best American Poetry*, series editor, David Lehman.

Stanza one contains letters, words, and line fragments from poems in the 2018 edition written by Allison Adair, Kaveh Akbar, Maryann Corbett, Sonia Greenfield, Terrance Hayes, Robin Coste Lewis, and Jessica Piazza.

Stanza two's sources are poems from the 2008 edition written by Robert Bly, Laura Cronk, Lydia Davis, Brenda Hillman, Mark Jarman, George Kalamaras, and Alex Lemon.

Stanza three is taken from poems found in the 1992 edition by Daniel Halpern, Robert Hass, Daniel Hoffman, Richard Howard, Lawrence Joseph, Jack Gilbert, Charles Bernstein, Elizabeth Bishop, and Susan Firer.

Stanza four is a cross-out of a poem by Nicky Beer from the 2007 edition.

Stanza five is taken from poems in the 2012 edition by Eduardo C. Corral, James Allen Hall, Sarah Lindsay, Elaine Equi, and Kerrin McCadden.

Lines 1-2a of stanza six are taken from poems in the 2011 edition by Jennifer Grotz, Allison Joseph, and James Richardson. Lines 2b-4 of stanza six are taken from poems in the 1994 edition by Dick Allen, Tom Andrews, John Ashbery, Ramola Dharmaraj, Thomas M. Disch, Brigit Pegeen Kelly, and Mark Doty.

Stanza seven is taken from poems in the 1993 edition by A. R. Ammons, Stephen Berg, Killarney Clary, Billy Collins, Barbara Cully, Carl Dennis, David Ignatow, Pamela Kircher, and Gerald Stern.

Stanza eight is taken from poems in the 1990 edition by Hayden Carruth, Anne Carson, Amy Gerstler, Donald Hall, Robert Hass, Emily Hiestand, John Hollander, Virginia Hooper, Lynne McMahon, and Jane Mead.

About the Author

Terry Lucas is the author of two prize-winning chapbooks, *If They Have Ears to Hear* (Southeast Missouri State University Press, 2012) and *Altar Call* (San Gabriel Valley Literary Festival, 2013), in addition to three previous full-length collections: *In This Room* (CW Books, 2016), *Dharma Rain* (Saint Julian Press, 2016), and with photographer Gary Topper, *The Thing Itself* (Longship Press, 2020).

His poetry has appeared in numerous national journals, including *Alaska Quarterly Review, Best New Poets,* and *The Sun.* Terry is Poet Laureate Emeritus of Marin County California and a freelance poetry coach at www.terrylucas.com.

www.ingramcontent.com/pod-product-compliance
Lightning Source LLC
Chambersburg PA
CBHW031153160426
43193CB00008B/348